IF I WERE A
PARK RANGER

CATHERINE STIER

ILLUSTRATED BY
PATRICK CORRIGAN

ALBERT WHITMAN & COMPANY
CHICAGO, ILLINOIS

Imagine serving as a park ranger for our US national parks!
If I were a national park ranger, after going to college to study wildlife biology, conservation, or education, I'd work for the National Park Service. I'd wear a special uniform, a hat, and a badge.

REDWOOD NATIONAL PARK, CA

If I were a national park ranger, I'd be part of what historian Wallace Stegner called America's "best idea." I'd proudly continue the legacy begun by people who had a vision of preserving our country's most beautiful, historic, and unique areas.

STEPHEN MATHER AND HORACE ALBRIGHT
The founding directors of the National Park Service

CAPTAIN CHARLES YOUNG
The first African American
superintendent of a national park

JOHN D. ROCKEFELLER JR.
With his family's millions, he funded the
creation and expansion of new parks.

THEODORE ROOSEVELT
As 26th President, he created programs to protect land, wildlife, and national treasures.

MARJORY STONEMAN DOUGLAS
Writer and conservationist who helped save the Everglades.

JOHN MUIR
His writings led to the establishment of Yosemite National Park in 1890.

GERARD BAKER
As superintendent, he brought Native American heritage and perspectives to the parks.

ANSEL ADAMS
His photographs captured the beauty of the national parks for the world to see.

Some people hang pictures of pretty scenery on their office walls. But if I were a national park ranger, I would spend my workday in a place that was beautiful all on its own.

If I were a national park ranger, I might work in the mountains,

OLYMPIC NATIONAL PARK, WA

in a cave,

MAMMOTH CAVE NATIONAL PARK

near a volcano,

HAWAI'I VOLCANOES NATIONAL PARK, HI

in the desert,

SAGUARO NATIONAL PARK, AZ

or at the seashore.

CANAVERAL NATIONAL SEASHORE, FL

Maybe I'd work on a ship or at a battlefield,

SAN FRANCISCO MARITIME NATIONAL HISTORICAL PARK, CA

GETTYSBURG NATIONAL MILITARY PARK, PA

near the homeland of an ancient people,
or at a famous national monument.

MESA VERDE NATIONAL PARK, CO

STATUE OF LIBERTY NATIONAL MONUMENT, NY

If I were a national park ranger, I would protect the land, the plants, the buildings, and the wild animals of my park.

PADRE ISLAND NATIONAL SEASHORE, TX

I'd protect animals in many ways. I'd make sure people didn't get too close to the animals or disturb their homes. I'd make sure people didn't feed them or leave garbage that might make the animals sick.

Protected spaces such as national parks and national seashores serve as living outdoor research laboratories. If I were a national park ranger, I might work with scientists to study the area's animals, plants, water, or soil. Or I could help with the discovery of fossils or artifacts in my park.

I'd help campers, hikers, sightseers, and other visitors to learn about and enjoy my park. Did you know that hundreds of millions of people visit National Park Service sites each year?

I might greet guests at the visitor center or lead a ranger talk. I'd meet people from all over the country and the world who traveled to see the treasures of the park.

YOSEMITE VISITOR CENTER

YOSEMITE NATIONAL PARK, CA

I'd be a great storyteller. I'd learn about the natural history, the human history, and the legends of my park so I could share those tales.

PETROGLYPH NATIONAL MONUMENT, NM

I'd tell a few spooky campfire stories too.

I'd know lots about the park's landmarks, plants, and wildlife. I'd even recognize the calls, tracks, and scat of most animals in my park, so I could answer any question—almost.

I might take people on a tour— on foot, in a tram, or in a kayak.

DE SOTO NATIONAL MEMORIAL, FL

Or maybe I'd lead a tour on snowshoes or by flashlight or even by candlelight! Lots of different knowledge and interests could come in handy.

GLACIER NATIONAL PARK, MT

I might dress up in old-fashioned clothes and portray someone from another time.

LINCOLN BOYHOOD NATIONAL MEMORIAL, IN

If I were a national park ranger, I'd always be on the lookout for fires or threatening weather. If I spotted trouble, I'd use my two-way radio to report it to the emergency dispatcher. Then the other rangers and I would use our training and experience to keep everyone and everything as safe as possible.

ACADIA NATIONAL PARK, ME

But sometimes, things still go wrong. Then I might be part of a search and rescue team that saves someone who is lost or in danger.

DEATH VALLEY NATIONAL PARK, CA, NV

If I were a park ranger, I'd probably spend time outside—maybe lots of time outside, in all kinds of different weather.

But park rangers work inside too. Some use computers to design exhibits, make maps, write articles, and keep track of endangered animal populations. Others update park websites with information and alerts about closed roads or other issues.

GREAT SMOKY MOUNTAINS NATIONAL PARK, NC, TN

If I were a national park ranger, I might leave my park to visit classrooms. I'd talk with students about the wonders of my workplace—because our national parks belong to them too.

If I were a national park ranger, my park would be cleaner and safer because of me. The animals living there would be stronger and healthier too.

CHANNEL ISLANDS NATIONAL PARK, CA

And maybe, because of all I did, some visitors to my park would experience something *astonishing*...

...a moment that could happen *nowhere else in the world.*

A moment they'd remember forever.

Then, like me, they'd want to take care of these very special places too.

GRAND CANYON NATIONAL PARK, AZ

So, yeah, I think someday I just might be a national park ranger.

MOUNT RUSHMORE NATIONAL MEMORIAL, SD

AUTHOR'S NOTE

I visited my first national park—the Great Smoky Mountains—when I was a baby. Later, my family made several car trips from Michigan to this beautiful place. We hiked to waterfalls, explored the mist-crowned mountains, picnicked by a rocky stream, and even spotted a bear. And…we met park rangers! Imagine working in such a beautiful and special place, I thought.

When I grew up, I visited the Grand Canyon, the Grand Tetons, Yellowstone, Yosemite, Carlsbad Caverns, the Statue of Liberty, and many other national park sites. Every park experience has been memorable and enhanced by the park rangers who provided security, information, interpretations, and even entertainment. This book is, in part, a tribute to them.

While researching this book, I have also learned the riches of our national parks go far beyond the often stunning scenery and the important conservation work many people associate with the parks. For example:

SCIENCE, TECHNOLOGY, ENGINEERING, AND MATH IN THE PARKS

National parks are innovative research laboratories. At Padre Island National Seashore in Texas, for example, the Sea Turtle Science and Recovery team conducts research, including the use of satellite tracking technology, to gather information that is studied to support five different species of endangered/threatened sea turtles. At other parks, engineering comes into play in the preservation of historic structures and monuments including the Statue of Liberty, as well as the planning and creation of roads and buildings such as visitor centers and dining and lodging facilities.

ART IN THE PARKS

Many national parks nurture guests' creativity and foster the creation of new works of art. At the Weir Farm National Historic Site, visitors may borrow art supplies to paint the landscape in this lovely rural Connecticut park. Some parks, such as the Rocky Mountains, offer ranger-led sketching and journaling hikes. Many parks host artist-in-residence programs, in which writers, musicians, and artists stay at the park, create original art reflective of the park, and often offer writing, painting, or music lessons or demonstrations for visitors.

DID YOU KNOW?

The visitor centers, museums, protected structures, and research libraries of our national parks are rich with preserved artifacts and primary source materials including documents, films, and photographs. Writers, filmmakers, scientists, historians, and conservationists visit national parks each year to conduct research, deepen their understanding of important subjects, and gather knowledge and material for their work. Students do too—one group of third and fourth graders, organized by the Pennsylvania Writing and Literature Project, studied primary sources at the Valley Forge National Historical Park to learn and write about the little-known stories of the African American soldiers who fought in the Revolutionary War.

My hope is that you will visit a national park site—or several—and discover for yourself all there is to learn, to see, and to experience. Our national parks truly are treasures to be enjoyed, valued, and protected.

SO WHAT DOES IT TAKE TO BE A PARK RANGER?

To become a park ranger for the National Park Service, you must be a US citizen. Having a college degree in history, wildlife management, ecology, parks management, or another related field is helpful.

Some park rangers work only seasonally, during the times of year when the parks are busiest. Others have specialized roles in law enforcement, search and rescue, or interpretation. In smaller parks, a park ranger may take on responsibilities in all these categories. Some park rangers live at the parks where they work, in cabins or dorm-like facilities. Once hired, a park ranger recruit may be sent to a National Park Service's training facility at the Grand Canyon, Harpers Ferry, or other locations.

The National Parks Service also employs people who are *not* park rangers. These staff members include park guides, science technicians, or archaeologists.

The parks welcome volunteers too! Volunteer opportunities for families and young people range from trail cleanup to dressing up in costume and portraying people from another time in living history programs.

Finally, kids may become Junior Rangers at many national parks. For more information, visit your favorite park's website or go to nps.gov/kids/become-a-junior-ranger.htm.

Acknowledgments

Thank you to all the National Park Service rangers who answered my many questions about our astonishing national parks and the responsibilities and rewards of a career as a park ranger. Much appreciation to Christina Cantrill of the National Writing Project for information on the students' Valley Forge National Historical Park research, and to fellow Texas author Patricia Vermillion for reviewing this manuscript. Finally, to those who shared in the vision and the adventure of creating a book set in our national parks and brought along their skill, insight, and enthusiasm—illustrator Patrick Corrigan, editor Wendy McClure, designer Ellen Kokontis, and the team at Albert Whitman—thank you!

To our dedicated park rangers with admiration and appreciation, and to those who have explored a national park with me—Mom, Dad, Janet, Mark, Chris, Linda, Randy, Andrew, and Julia—CS

For my awesome nephew and nieces: George, Edie, Eloisa, and Genevieve—PC

Library of Congress Cataloging-in-Publication data is on file with the publisher.

Text copyright © 2019 by Catherine Stier
Illustrations copyright © 2019 by Albert Whitman & Company
Illustrations by Patrick Corrigan
Hardcover edition first published in the United States of America in 2019 by Albert Whitman & Company
Paperback edition first published in the United States of America in 2022 by Albert Whitman & Company
ISBN 978-0-8075-3548-6 (paperback)
ISBN 978-0-8075-3546-2 (ebook)

Printed in China
10 9 8 7 6 5 4 3 WKT 28 27 26 25 24

For more information about Albert Whitman & Company,
visit our website at www.albertwhitman.com.